P9-CQZ-369

3 3090 00269 8241

The Library of Physics™

KINETIC AND POTENTIAL ENERGY
Understanding Changes Within Physical Systems

Jennifer Viegas

The Rosen Publishing Group, Inc., New York

Fremont Public Library
1170 N. Midlothian Road
Mundelein, IL 60060

Published in 2005 by The Rosen Publishing Group, Inc.
29 East 21st Street, New York, NY 10010

Copyright © 2005 by The Rosen Publishing Group, Inc.

First Edition

All rights reserved. No part of this book may be reproduced in any form without permission in writing from the publisher, except by a reviewer.

Library of Congress Cataloging-in-Publication Data

Viegas, Jennifer.
Kinetic and potential energy : understanding changes within physical systems/by Jennifer Viegas for the Rosen Publishing Group.—1st ed.
    p. cm.—(The library of physics)
Includes bibliographical references.
ISBN 1-4042-0333-8 (lib. bdg.)
1. Force and energy. 2. Dynamics. 3. Energy transfer.
I. Title. II. Series: Library of physics (Rosen Publishing Group)
QC73.V54 2005
531'.6—dc22

                                    2004019126
Manufactured in the United States of America

On the cover: A Newton's cradle, a popular physics toy that consists of a set of steel balls suspended from a frame. The law of inertia, conservation of momentum, and Newton's third law can be observed in the motion and collisions of the balls of the Newton's cradle system.

Contents

Introduction   4

1 Potential and Kinetic Energy   11

2 Mechanical Energy   20

3 The Laws of Energy   28

4 Momentum   35

Glossary   43

For More Information   45

For Further Reading   46

Bibliography   46

Index   47

Introduction

Physics is the study of matter, energy, and motion. Since everything in our world relates to these three basic subjects, physics can help you understand many working systems in the universe. Incredibly, the same universal laws that apply to playing basketball or to achieving success in other sports can also apply to how airplanes fly, space shuttles take off, and planets orbit. At first, it might seem difficult to see any connection between how a pro basketball star wins a game and how the solar system moves, but the same physics principles apply. It all comes down to energy and matter.

Matter and Energy

The universe consists of matter and energy. Matter can be thought of as the stuff that energy acts upon. Take a look at your surroundings. This book is matter, as are your desk, pen, and clothing. Rocks, water, plants, animals, and even you are made up of matter. Earth is made of matter, as are all of the other stars and planets.

Universal laws of physics explain the motion of all objects, including this airplane and truck. Motion is a function of energy. The energy used to propel the engines of vehicles comes from fossil fuels that are burned to produce heat.

Energy is a harder concept to understand. You cannot always see energy when it is present. Energy is what makes things happen. Imagine what the world would be like without it. Nothing could breathe or move. Plants could not grow. You would not be able to function. The oceans would never have waves. The stars would not appear to come out at night. Matter without energy would mean that our world would be a very dull, inactive place where nothing happens.

Usually you cannot see energy. You only see what it does. You may think that you see energy in the form of gasoline, electrical wires, or batteries, but these really are just substances and objects that have the ability to release energy. What is energy? Scientists define it as the capacity to do work. In other words, energy causes change and makes things happen.

The Sun: Our Energy Supplier

Most of the energy on Earth comes from one source, the Sun. If you stand outside on a sunny day, you can actually see and feel its energy. That is because the Sun's energy is released in two main ways: light and heat. From the food that fuels us to the electricity that powers our television sets and computers, most energy used by humans began as light emitted by the Sun.

Although you may feel warm and get a tan after standing outside on a sunny day, your body can only convert some of the Sun's rays into usable energy. Flowers, trees, and other plants take care of most of the conversion. Without them, almost all of the Sun's energy would flow past Earth and would not cause anything to occur. Every living thing on our planet benefits from the process plants use to convert Sun energy into food energy. This process is called photosynthesis.

During photosynthesis, light energy from the Sun is trapped in plant chloroplasts. The plant then combines the energy with water and carbon dioxide to make sugar, which serves as food, or energy, for the plant.

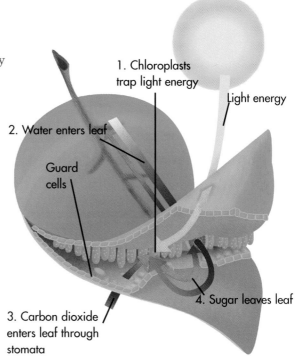

1. Chloroplasts trap light energy

Light energy

2. Water enters leaf

Guard cells

3. Carbon dioxide enters leaf through stomata

4. Sugar leaves leaf

Photosynthesis

Green plants can trap the Sun's light energy in a green substance called chlorophyll. As the Sun shines down on plants, the chlorophyll absorbs the light as energy. The word used to describe this process is "photosynthesis."

Plants combine light energy with water and carbon dioxide, a gas that is present in the air around us, to make a simple sugar. All green plants, whether or not they taste sweet, contain some form of sugar. Some plants use the sugar to make other kinds of food, such as starches and fats. The food helps to nourish the plants. It also helps to nourish animals, including humans.

Even when we eat meat, we are getting nutrition that once existed in plants. Somewhere along the food chain, an animal got its food from a plant source. A chicken, for example, might eat bugs that ate plants. When we eat chicken, fish, or any kind of meat, we benefit from the food that originally came from a plant source.

Fossil Fuels

Humans and other living things gain energy by eating food. Cars, planes, computers, televisions, and most other equipment and machines get their energy either directly or indirectly from fossil fuels. Just as the energy in food can be traced back to sunlight, so, too, can the energy in fossil fuels. Gasoline, petroleum oil, coal, natural gas, and other forms of energy called fossil fuels get their name from the fact that they developed from the fossilized remains of prehistoric plants and animals. The fuel used to run a car is processed from substances that were originally plants and animals. These plants or animals could have lived during the age of dinosaurs, or even millions of years before that.

Over 80 percent of the world's energy, including electricity, comes from fossil fuels. Many large power plants that produce electricity get their energy from coal. You probably do not realize that every time you

Fossil fuels located deep in the ground often are brought to the surface by means of heavy metal drills. Fossil fuels are produced by the decay of ancient, fossilized animals and plants. The process takes up to millions of years.

use an electrical appliance, a power plant likely burns coal to create heat energy. The heat boils water to create steam. The steam then rushes through a machine that spins very fast. The spinning produces electricity that wires transport over long distances. When you plug in anything that runs on electricity, you are tapping into this electrical energy.

Fossil fuels are in limited supply because it takes thousands, even millions, of years for plants to turn into coal, petroleum, and natural gas. Burning fossil fuels also produces pollution that can create smog and smoke, which may lead to environmental and health problems. Despite the gradually dwindling supply of fossil fuels and the potential risks of using them, the demand for fossil fuels has doubled every twenty years since 1900.

Scientists now are looking for renewable sources of energy, which are sources that will never run out, or will not run out for a very long time. Most of these sources rely more directly on the Sun's energy. Solar power, for example, can be collected by man-made cells that somewhat copy the way plant cells gather light energy from the Sun.

Potential and Kinetic Energy

By themselves, food and fuel seem to possess little, if any, energy. Unless you move them, a bowl of fruit and a container full of gasoline will have no motion and no apparent life to them. If you eat the fruit, however, you will have the energy to move. If someone pumps gas into a car tank, he or she provides the car energy for driving. Food and gas are two examples of substances that contain potential energy.

Potential Energy

At some point, you probably have heard a friend, family member, or even yourself described as having "a lot of potential," usually in reference to ability. This means that the person with potential has not achieved his or her full level of success yet, but that the individual possesses the ability to excel in the future. That is what potential energy is like. Potential energy is the stored energy of an object, which depends on its position, rather than its motion. For this reason, potential energy is also known as the energy of position. This stored energy means that the object has the potential to work. In other words, the stored energy can be released.

To see how potential energy works, try this experiment. Place a rubber band in front of you. Unless you move it, the rubber band will stay where it is. Now, place the rubber band over the tip of your index finger and pull back on it with the thumb and index finger of your other hand. You have just given the rubber band potential energy. As long as you hold the rubber band in that outstretched position, it has the potential to move. Be sure that no one is in front of you and that nothing breakable is in the rubber band's path before you release it.

Elastic Potential Energy

A rubber band is an example of elastic potential energy. This kind of energy can be stored in materials that may be stretched or compressed. Daredevils make use of this kind of energy when they jump while tied to a bungee cord. Using special equipment and with the help of professionals, bungee jumpers leap off bridges and other high places. When the jumper reaches the bottom of the jump, potential energy that has built up in the cord will jolt the jumper back up into the air.

Trampolines also use elastic potential energy. The material stretched out on the trampoline acts like a rubber band. When you jump down on it, you give the material stored energy. It then has the potential to bounce you back upward. Springs

This group of professional soccer players uses giant rubber bands in their strength training program. The bands provide constant resistance as long as they are held taut. The stretched rubber bands contain potential energy to propel the athletes forward. The athletes build strength by pushing against this potential energy.

operate in almost the same way, except they can also be compressed, or squashed down. The compression gives them potential energy.

Chemical Potential Energy

Another kind of potential energy is chemical. Until recently, not much was understood about chemical potential energy. However, recent advances in the physics of very small particles have enabled scientists to better learn what kind of energy exists on an atomic scale. Bonds between atoms store potential energy. Electrons (tiny subatomic particles that carry a negative electrical charge) and electronic charge differences are what form the bonds. Electrons themselves do not provide any potential energy. Only the bonds between atoms exist as a source of potential energy. Food, batteries, gas, and coal are all examples of chemical potential energy.

When you eat a piece of fruit, for example, your digestive system works on the fruit to break down the nutrients stored within it. If you have not eaten in a while and are active, your body might use this energy right away to help fuel your actions. If not, the fruit's energy could be stored for future use. That is one reason why eating a lot can cause weight gain. Your body stores all of the extra energy as fat, which itself becomes a source of chemical potential energy within your body.

Calories

You probably know that a candy bar has more calories than a small piece of fruit, but do you know exactly what a calorie is? A calorie is a measurement of how much heat energy is contained in food. When we "burn" calories, we are using up the food's energy. Humans burn calories all of the time. Even sitting still reading this book will burn about 100 calories an hour. That is because your body is maintaining its temperature, your heart is beating, you are breathing, and other bodily activities are taking place, such as blinking and turning the pages.

More than half of the United States' electricity supply is generated from burning coal. The United States produces one-fifth of the global supply of coal.

Gravitational Potential Energy

Yet another form of potential energy comes from gravity, which is the pull that all objects of mass have on each other. Mass is the amount of matter that a living or nonliving thing has. On Earth, your mass is equal to your weight. If you were to travel to the Moon, your mass would stay the same, but your weight would change. That is because on Earth your weight is a measurement of your gravitational

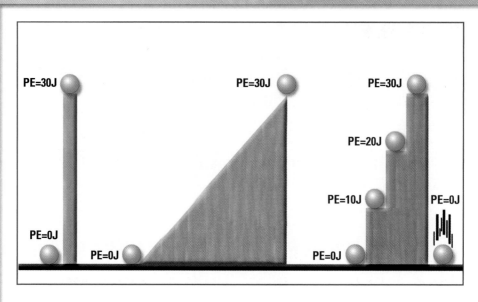

Position gives these balls potential energy. At the same height, the top three balls have potential energy equal to 30 joules. That amount decreases as the height decreases. The balls on the ground have no height, and therefore they have zero joules of potential energy.

attraction to Earth and Earth's gravitational attraction to you. If you weigh 100 pounds (45.36 kilograms) on Earth, you would weigh slightly more than 17.64 pounds (8 kg) on the Moon because the effect of the Moon's gravity is less than that of Earth's.

When you pick up an object, such as an eraser, you give it gravitational potential energy. When you let it go, it will fall to the ground because of gravity. By lifting it up, you give it the potential to move.

Gravitational potential energy, therefore, is the energy stored within an object due to its vertical position, or height. To determine an object's gravitational energy, three facts must be known: the object's mass, its height, and the acceleration of gravity. On Earth, the acceleration of gravity is equal to 32 feet per second squared, or 32 ft/s^2. When these three data points are factored together, a formula is created for calculating gravitational potential energy. The formula is PE (gravitational) = mgh, where m stands for mass, g stands for acceleration of gravity, and h stands for height.

Joule

Another symbol associated with potential energy is "J." It stands for "joule," which is a unit of measurement in the metric system used to measure work or energy. One joule is equal to the amount of work done when one newton, or 0.225 pounds (0.1 kg) of force, moves an object 3 feet (1 meter) in the direction of the force. Since joules are also used to measure all kinds of energy, including heat energy,

This skier has energy of position due to his raised level on the mountainside. The descent involves kinetic energy, or energy of motion.

joules can be used in place of calories. One joule is equal to 0.239 calories.

Kinetic Energy

Kinetic energy is the energy that something has when it is in motion. You can often see and feel this energy. If you place a rubber band on a pillow, it will not create much of a dent, but if you shoot the rubber band into the pillow, its force will leave a dent. If you have ever been struck by a rubber band, a baseball, or some other object, you know how strong kinetic energy can be. That is because the potential energy of these objects was released into the kinetic energy of motion.

The formula used to calculate kinetic energy is KE = (mass x velocity^2)/2, which can also be written as KE = $1/2 mv^2$. Kinetic energy, then, is equal to one-half the mass of an object times its velocity squared. Velocity, in turn, is speed (distance divided by time) with a direction.

Unlike potential energy, there is only one form of kinetic energy, but different types of motion can exemplify kinetic energy. Three of these types of motion are vibrational, rotational, and translational. Vibrational energy is the energy that something has when it vibrates, which is a form of movement. A drum head or a metal cooking pan that has just been hit, for example, might have a vibrating energy that you can feel.

Rotational energy can be felt if you spin a top on a flat surface. If you feel around the sides of the top without touching it, you might detect a slight breeze. That is air being moved around by the rotational energy created by the spinning top. A similar effect happens when Earth rotates. The

A spinning top has rotational energy, which is a type of motion that exemplifies kinetic energy.

atmosphere above Earth can move in response to Earth's circular rotation.

Translational kinetic energy is the energy due to movement from one place to another. It is a very common example of kinetic energy. If you move from one part of a room to another, you will experience translational kinetic energy while you are moving. When you stop moving, you go back to having potential energy because you retain the potential to move again. In this way, potential and kinetic energy go hand in hand.

2 Mechanical Energy

Kinetic and potential energy make up what is known as mechanical energy. Mechanical energy is energy that an object has because of its motion or because of its energy stored as a result of position. Sometimes objects with mechanical energy possess both kinetic and potential energy at the same time. For example, a Frisbee flying through the air has kinetic energy of motion. The moving Frisbee also flies above the ground, which gives it gravitational potential energy.

If you lift this book over your head, you have just given the book mechanical energy. When it is above the ground, the book has gravitational potential energy. You can even do the same thing to a single page in the book. If you lift a page up, it has potential energy. If you let go of the page, it will fall down due to gravity. When you lifted the page, you performed work on it.

Work

Like the words "potential" and "energy," "work" is one of those terms that you probably think you know but may not fully understand. In physics, the word

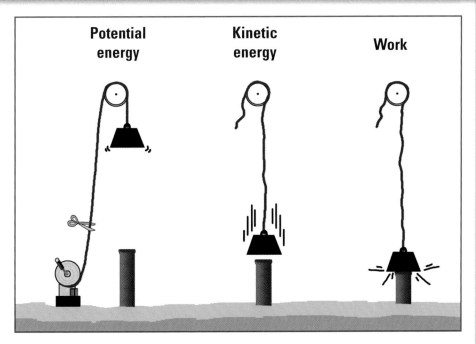

Potential energy

Kinetic energy

Work

On the left, the raised weight has potential energy. When the rope holding the weight in place over the pulley is cut, the weight has kinetic energy, an energy of motion. As the weight falls and pushes down on the bar, the weight performs work.

"work" refers to a force that acts upon an object to cause a displacement, meaning that the object moves or changes in some way from its original state. Whenever work occurs, there must be some force, or source of energy, to initiate the process. When you turn the pages of this book, the energy derived from food that you ate creates the necessary force.

Force can be defined as power, or energy, exerted on any person or thing. Force often refers to a push or a pull on something. The amount of force is used to calculate work. Work equals force times distance moved, or $W = fd$. Work is measured in foot-pounds or joules. The joule equals 0.7 foot-pounds. Turning book pages does not require much force. Other activities require more energy. At times, your book bag may weigh a lot, so you have to use a fair amount of force to lift it up. If your book bag weighs 25 pounds (11 kg) and you raise it from a height of 3 feet to 5 feet (0.9 to 1.5 meters), you will have done 50 foot-pounds, or 35 joules, of work. That is because the work is equal to 25 times 2. The force in this case is equal to the weight of the book bag.

Kinetic energy also sometimes has the ability to transform itself into potential energy, which can then go back to kinetic energy to create a continuous cycle. Many gadgets and machines take advantage of this process because the cycle requires only an initial force to get things going. Watches, playground swings, and roller coasters all operate by alternating potential with kinetic energy.

How Pendulums Work

A pendulum is a suspended object that is free to move between two extremes. Grandfather clocks usually use a pendulum to drive the clocks' mechanisms. The height of the pendulum bob above its lowest point determines its potential energy. The central position between swings is its lowest point. As the bob lifts, it has both kinetic and potential energy. When it reaches its highest position above the lowest point, the bob contains only potential energy. At the bob's lowest point when it is about to swing in the other direction, it contains only kinetic energy. This system of mechanical energy causes the clock to do work. The total energy of the pendulum is constant and is just changing back and forth between kinetic and potential energy.

Even a human can act like a pendulum bob. When you sit on a swing, you are at the lowest point of the possible swing arc. To start a swing, potential energy within your body switches to kinetic energy to move you forward and upward. At

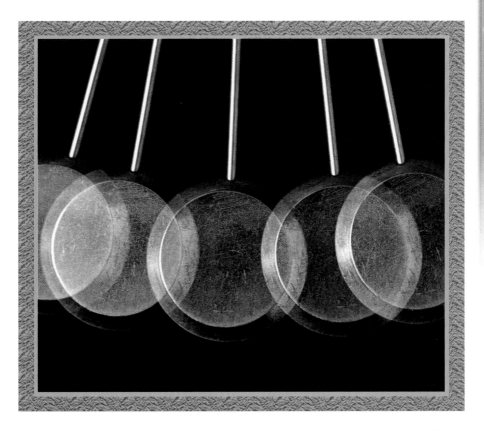

A pendulum maintains constant energy because kinetic and potential energy change back and forth in equal amounts.

the highest point of the swing arc, you then become like a pendulum bob at its highest point. In that instant, only potential energy exists if you remain motionless. The potential energy then quickly changes to kinetic energy and you can swing back downward without any effort on your part. If you continued to just sit in the swing without exerting a force, eventually you would stop going back and forth. You do not swing forever because of friction and air resistance.

Friction and Air Resistance

Friction is a force that opposes, or goes against, motion. It occurs whenever two or more objects with irregular surfaces interact. The interaction causes the surfaces to bump, slide, and scrape against each other, which slows down, or stops, motion. Air resistance acts in a similar way. It serves as a frictional force against objects that move through air, such as a pendulum bob or a person on a swing.

How Roller Coasters Work

Roller coasters make clever use of mechanical energy. Although you can travel at very high speeds on a roller coaster, the cars of most coasters do not have engines. Only an initial force, created by an external engine at the beginning of the ride, sets the kinetic-potential cycle in motion.

At the beginning of a roller-coaster ride, a machine of some kind uses force to pull the coaster car up a hill. A rider sitting in a coaster car at the

Air can resist force, but it can also serve as a force itself. Here, windmills get their energy from the wind.

Why Car Tires Have Treads

If you look at tires on a car, you will see that they have a raised surface of rubber on them. This surface actually promotes friction. It helps the car to better grip the road. Whenever the treads wear down, people have to buy new tires because driving without this friction can be dangerous. A car without good treads on a wet surface, for example, could slide and cause a crash. Race car tires do not have treads. Race car drivers sacrifice safety for speed, and they also drive in a more controlled environment.

top of a hill now has gravitational potential energy. The higher the hill, the greater the potential energy will be. The coaster's motion, created by the initial force, and the weight of the ride will then cause the coaster cars and their contents to plummet downward. As the coaster moves, it has kinetic energy. Sometimes this movement will be divided into loops, which can whirl riders around and around in circles. The rotational energy of the loops combines kinetic and potential energy, so the coaster keeps going.

During the ride, the roller coaster transforms energy from one form to another. With each climb, the roller coaster's kinetic energy decreases and its gravitational potential energy increases. With each descent, gravitational potential decreases and kinetic energy increases.

If it were possible to design a giant roller coaster across all of the continents, a ride could potentially go on forever converting potential energy into kinetic energy were it not for friction, such as that from the coaster's wheels against the tracks. In fact, imposed friction is what ultimately causes most roller coasters to come to a full stop. Compressed air brakes create friction underneath the cars, and this friction is sufficient to stop the ride's motion.

Most machines at school and in your home take somewhat similar advantage of the cyclical nature of kinetic and potential energy. Refrigerators continuously circulate coolant to suck heat out of foods stored in the refrigerator. Hairdryers use electricity to initiate motions within the dryer to heat and move air. When a hairdryer is not plugged into an electrical outlet, it does not have any potential energy that can be used to dry your hair. When it is plugged in and turned on, electricity gives the hairdryer the potential to heat and blow your hair. As the hairdryer works, it has both potential and kinetic energy.

Even hand-operated tools, like manual can openers, use human potential energy to run the mechanics of the tool. By itself, a can opener would remain motion-less were it not for a person's conversion of his or her potential energy into kinetic energy, which initiates the operation of the device.

3 The Laws of Energy

M achines may vary in size, but the same laws of energy govern how they operate. This is similar to how you compare with your classmates. Everyone is different, but on a basic level you function in the same manner. Doctors use these similarities to understand their patients. Similarly, physicists use the laws of energy to understand many different kinds of systems that exist both here on Earth and throughout the universe. One of the most important of these laws is called the conservation of energy.

Conservation of Energy

The law of conservation of energy holds that there is a fixed amount of energy in the entire universe. This amount can never change. That means energy can never be created or destroyed. We merely change energy from one form to another. For fossil fuels, the amount of energy that plants originally used to create the potential energy in the fuels equals the sum of all of the forms of energy that are given up when the fuels are burned.

To understand the law of conservation of energy, consider the transformations of energy that occur after you exercise or do some chores around the house. Your body converts food into energy that enables you to become active. This energy is released as kinetic energy when you move. The amount of energy from the food you eat, however, is not equal to your kinetic energy of movement. A lot of the energy is released as heat, which itself is a form of

As this jogger runs, his body converts potential energy into kinetic energy of motion. Changes from one form of energy to another are called energy conversions.

energy. That is one reason why you feel hot after you run for a while. Your body burns more calories than necessary for your movement and releases the extra energy as heat.

Since heat is energy, heat is conserved, too. For example, at lunchtime, you might place a hot bowl of soup on the table. If you go away for a while to take a phone call or to do something else, when you return, the soup will be colder than it was before, unless the room was the same temperature as the soup. That is because heat from the soup, released in steam, leaves the soup and is absorbed by air in the room. Since the room is much bigger than the bowl of soup, you likely will not be able to feel any difference in the room's temperature, but the heat energy never completely went away.

Systems have a tendency toward increasing disorder. This tendency is known as entropy, which also may be defined as the degree to which energy within a system is unavailable for conversion into work. When you turn on a light, for example, the electrical energy used to run it results in light and heat. If you have the light on for a while, you can feel the heat if you place your hand next to the lightbulb. This heat will be absorbed by the air in the room. Ordered

Humans Generate a Lot of Heat

When you are sick, you might feel warm if you have a fever. Even when you are healthy and not active, chemical energy in your body is partly released as heat. That is why a normal person has a temperature of 98.6° Fahrenheit (37° Celsius) instead of zero. Although you might not realize it, when you are in a classroom with only nine other students, the ten of you create heat equal to a blazing fire. You do not feel the heat as you would near a fire because it is dispersed around the classroom.

energy, such as the electricity that you desire to power the light, also results in this disordered energy, the waste heat that is released in most processes. Physicists are currently seeking ways to limit waste heat or to convert it back into ordered energy.

The Work-Energy Theorem

Work and energy go together because you cannot have one without the other. It takes energy to create work, and work will never happen without some kind of force. It is possible to figure out how much work has been done by using the work-energy theorem. This theorem states that the net, or total, work performed on an object is equal to the change in the object's kinetic energy. As an equation this is stated as $fd = 1/2mv^2$, where force times distance, equals one-half the product of mass times velocity squared.

Many factors can change an object's kinetic energy. Imagine a football on a sidewalk. It gets kinetic energy if you kick it or throw it, someone on a bicycle bangs into it, causing it to move, or a strong wind blows it around. When left alone, however, the football tends to stay put. That tendency to not change without force is called inertia.

The Law of Inertia

An English scientist named Sir Isaac Newton (1642–1727) created several laws that help explain motion. His first law of motion states that if an object is at rest, it wants to stay that way. If an object is

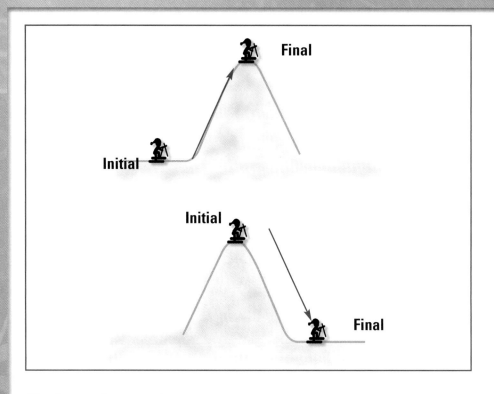

The forces of gravity, friction, and air resistance act on the skier. Without these forces, total mechanical energy would be conserved and the skier would travel forever. As the skier goes up the hill, height and potential energy increases and speed and kinetic energy decreases. The reverse happens when the skier goes down the hill. The total of kinetic and potential energy (mechanical energy) would not change were it not for the forces of gravity, friction, and air resistance.

moving, it will keep moving at a constant speed and in a constant direction unless a force changes that.

Because of inertia, you should be able to kick the football and make it move forever. That does not happen, of course. The pull of gravity, friction, and air resistance eventually causes the football to fall back to the ground. If you lessen these factors, the football, or any object, could travel over a great distance. Ice, for example, is smoother than a sidewalk. It lessens the amount of friction. That is why a hockey puck can slide across a skating rink after it has been struck by a hockey stick. Without the walls of the rink and if more ice were present, the puck could travel an enormous distance.

The Work-Energy Theorem of a Moving Bike

A bike pedaled forward illustrates the work-energy theorem. Imagine that you hop on a bike and pedal it forward over a distance of 0.46 meters (18 inches). Recall that energy is often measured in joules. One joule is equal to the amount of energy it takes to lift 0.45 kilograms (1 pound) 0.23 meters (9 in). If you weigh 45.36 kilograms (100 lbs.) and your bike weighs 13.61 kilograms, it would take around 130 joules to move the bike 0.23 meters (9 in). Since you moved forward twice that distance, double that amount of force, or 260 joules, could allow the bike to move forward.

If you have ever tried to bike up a hill, you know that it is not easy. A lot of forces work against you. The force of gravity wants to pull you and your bike down the hill. Friction caused by the hill's irregular surface creates a resistance, or a negative force, against your pedaling. If air is blowing in your face, that, too, can create a negative friction force. If the negative forces in this example add up to 40 joules, then the positive forces would have to be 300 joules for work to equal 260 joules. You would need the extra 40 joules to counteract the negative forces of

40 joules caused by gravity and friction.

To figure out the net work of any system, such as that of the bike moving uphill, first consider the kinetic energy that it has when moving from the starting point to the finishing point. Next, consider any other positive or negative forces that might occur along the way. If the wind was blowing in the direction that the biker was going in, it might be a positive force. The sum of all of these forces can then be used to calculate the net work done on the object.

These mountain bikers have to be in good physical condition to counteract the forces of gravity and friction and to move their bikes forward.

4

Momentum

nother word that you probably are familiar with is "momentum." A huge football player, for example, has a lot of momentum when he charges down a football field. Momentum is a measurement of the amount of inertia and motion that an object has. It is equal to an object's mass multiplied by its velocity. In equation form, this is written as $p = mv$, where p stands for momentum. A small car traveling at 30 miles (48.3 kilometers) per hour, therefore, has a lot less momentum than a large, heavy truck traveling at the same speed. Momentum also is a vector quantity, meaning that it has direction.

Conservation of Momentum

Like energy, momentum in a system is conserved—no momentum is gained, and none is lost. What would happen to the football player's momentum if he was running down the field and tackled by a player on the opposing team? At first, you might think that his momentum would be lost, but it really would be redirected toward the player who tackled

Assuming that they are both moving at the same speed, the car to the right has a lot less momentum than the heavier truck. Momentum is the mass of a moving object times its velocity.

him. That is why the tackler would feel the force of his impact.

As another example, imagine you are sitting in a motionless bumper car at an amusement park. The momentum at this point is zero. Your friend in another car comes at you with ten units of momentum. Upon impact, his momentum would be divided between the two cars. You would move with five units of momentum, and he would move forward with five units.

If your car is between two other bumper cars and each of these other cars comes at you from opposite directions, your car would not move. The force of one moving car would cancel out the force of the other moving car because momentum is a vector quantity and the two cars were coming from different directions. The total momentum in this case would be the same as it was at the outset: zero. If you are sitting in your bumper car and your friends both come from the same direction,

If the bumper car on the left bangs into the center bumper car, some of its momentum will be transferred to the center car, which would cause the center car to veer to the right.

one after another, you will all move and share in the force of impact.

The game of billiards takes advantage of the conservation of momentum. A neat trick based on momentum conservation is demonstrated when a pool player hits a ball toward a row of balls. The momentum of the first moving ball passes through several stationary balls and causes the last one in the row to move forward. Momentum is not lost. It is simply transferred from one ball to another, until finally the last ball in the row moves.

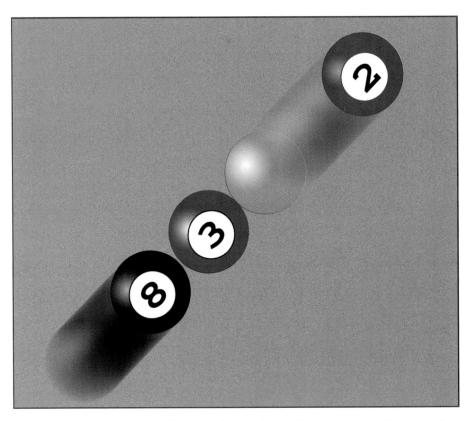

Although ball 3 is directly hit by ball 8, ball 2 will move due to the transfer of momentum from 3 to 2.

Because momentum has direction, it can transfer at different angles. For example, if a pool player hits a ball toward a V-shaped set of balls, balls from either side of the V will move forward at an equal pace. The momentum of the original ball is shared between them.

Make Physics Work for You

Now that you have learned some of the basic laws of energy and momentum, you can use them to your advantage. One day you might decide to become an airline pilot, a professional athlete, an inventor, or a musician. These careers, and more, all involve physics laws.

How Energy and Momentum Laws Can Help Athletes

If you have ever played basketball and jumped high toward the hoop, you know that when you hit the ground, the impact can be painful. If you increase the amount of time it takes for your body to reach the ground, you will lessen the impact. That is why pro basketball players always try to bend their knees while landing a jump. The bending slightly increases the time of impact and reduces the force that the impact has on their bodies. The higher the jump is, the greater the impact will be, so high-jumping pro players especially need to adjust their landing stance.

Karate experts who break boards with their hands do not care about the distance that the boards will travel. The time of impact between the martial artist's hand and the wood is very short. These experts change their potential energy into kinetic energy in a split second. They then transfer the force of their momentum to the wood board, which cracks upon collision. Only experienced karate professionals can do these tricks without risking injury.

To hit a golf ball a long distance, you also must lengthen the time of impact. The longer your club stays in contact with the ball, the greater the distance the ball will travel because more energy will be transferred from the club to the ball. Famous golf players spend countless hours perfecting their swings so they can transfer maximum momentum from their bodies to the ball via the club head. If the club becomes an extension of your arm, virtually all of the momentum from your swing will go toward the movement of the golf ball.

How Airplanes Stay in the Air

Energy and motion laws also help to explain how moving airplanes stay in the sky. In a well-maintained aircraft, passengers can rest easy because a balance of air pressure forces can keep an airplane flying indefinitely, so long as the plane has enough fuel to move in a forward direction.

The next time you travel on an airplane or visit an airport, notice the shape of the airplane's wings. They are slightly curved on the top. The curve causes air above the wing to travel a longer distance than it must travel below the wing, even though air rushes past the plane at an equal rate. The difference in air pressure created by the wing design gives lift to the lower part of the plane. Air holds the plane above the ground. The wings of birds and the shape of dolphins and whales also often have the curve design that an airplane wing has. This shape gives them lift in air and even in water.

From airplanes to rockets to computers, humans have invented all sorts of objects that operate based on the laws of energy, momentum, and motion. They all release heat as energy. When we use gasoline in cars and planes or use electricity to run appliances, we usually turn fossil fuels into heat and other particles, and also create usable energy. That is why the hood of a running car feels warm and exhaust

Turn Your Hand into an Airplane

When you are riding in a car on a stretch of road that is free of other cars, you might try this neat trick. Stretch your arm outside of the car window. At first hold your arm and hand straight across. Then, slightly lift your hand at the front. Your hand should start to rise a little. Just like an airplane, you have created a change in air pressure from the top to the bottom of your hand. Air lifts your hand up, just as it lifts planes up in the sky.

releases from the back. On average, only 25 percent of a car's gasoline actually works to move the car. The other 75 percent turns into heat energy.

One of the greatest challenges of your generation will be to design more energy-efficient cars, planes, and appliances, so that they will make better use of energy, release less pollution, and lose less energy as heat. Energy released from the Sun each year is more than 15,000 times what all humans use in that same time period. Solar energy may one day provide us with a clean, efficient form of energy. Its potential, as well as yours, for bringing about positive, kinetic change in our world is nearly limitless.

Glossary

chemical potential energy (KEH-mih-kul poh-TEN-shul EH-nur-jee) The energy stored within atomic bonds in substances.

conservation of energy (kon-sur-VAY-shun uv EH-nur-jee) The physics law that states that there is a fixed amount of energy in the entire universe and this amount can never change.

conservation of momentum (kon-sur-VAY-shun uv moh-MEN-tum) The physics law that states that the total momentum in a system does not change, even when objects collide.

elastic potential energy (ih-LAS-tik poh-TEN-shul EH-nur-jee) Energy that is stored in objects that can be stretched or compressed.

energy (EH-nur-jee) The capacity to do work; what causes change and makes things happen.

fossil fuels (FAH-sul FYOOLZ) Gas, coal, petroleum, and other products that are derived from the oily remains of prehistoric plants and animals.

friction (FRIK-shin) A force that opposes motion.

gravitational potential energy (gra-vih-TAY-shu-nul poh-TEN-shul EH-nur-jee) Stored energy that comes from gravity, which is the pull that all objects of mass have on each other.

inertia (ih-NUR-shah) The tendency of an object to remain at rest or in uniform motion in a straight line unless it is acted upon by an external force.

kinetic energy (kih-NEH-tik EH-nur-jee) The energy that an object has when it is in motion.

mass (MAS) The amount of matter that a living or nonliving thing has.

matter (MAT-tur) Anything that has mass and occupies space.

mechanical energy (mih-KA-nih-kul EH-nur-jee) Energy that an object has because of its motion, or its energy stored as a result of the object's position.

momentum (moh-MEN-tum) A measurement of the amount of inertia and motion that an object has that is equal to an object's mass multiplied by its velocity.

physics (FIH-ziks) The study of matter, energy, and motion.

potential energy (poh-TEN-shul EH-nur-jee) The energy that an object has because of its position or because of the arrangement of its parts.

renewable energies (ree-NOO-uh-bul EH-nur-jeez) Solar, wind, water, and other energy sources that are in constant supply, as opposed to energy sources such as fossil fuels that are available in limited amounts.

rotational kinetic energy (roh-TAY-shu-nul kih-NEH-tik EH-nur-jee) The kinetic energy of an object rotating around an axis.

translational kinetic energy (tranz-LAY-shu-nul kih-NEH-tik EH-nur-jee) The energy of an object moving in a straight line.

velocity (veh-LOS-ih-tee) A measurement of the speed and direction a moving object has.

vibrational kinetic energy (vy-BRAY-shu-nuh kih-NEH-tik EH-nur-jee) The kinetic energy of a vibrating object.

work (WURK) What occurs when a force that acts upon an object causes a displacement, meaning that the object moves or changes in some way from its original state.

work-energy theorem (WURK-EH-nur-jee THEE-uh-rum) A physics law that states that the net, or total, work done on an object is equal to the change in the object's kinetic energy.

For More Information

Physics Academic Software c/o PAS
940 Main Campus Drive, Suite 210
Raleigh, NC 27606-5212
(800) 955-8275 or (919) 829-8181
e-mail: pas@webassign.net
Web site: http://www.aip.org/pas

Physics Today Magazine
American Institute of Physics
Circulation and Fullfillment Division, Suite 1NO1
2 Huntington Quadrangle
Melville, NY 11747

The Society of Physics Students
American Institute of Physics
One Physics Ellipse
College Park, MD 20740

Web Sites

Due to the changing nature of Internet links, the Rosen
Publishing Group, Inc., has developed an online list of Web
sites related to the subject of this book. This site is updated
regularly. Please use this link to access the list:

http://www.rosenlinks.com/liph/kipe

For Further Reading

Dalton, Cindy Devine. *Force & Motion*. Vero Beach, FL: Rourke Publications, 2001.

Dalton, Cindy Devine. *Gravity*. Vero Beach, FL: Rourke Publications, 2001.

Farndon, John. *Gravity*. New York: Benchmark Books, 2002.

Hillerman, Anne. *Done in the Sun: Solar Projects for Children*. Santa Fe, NM: Sunstone Press, 1983.

Paul, Richard. *A Handbook to the Universe: Explorations of Matter, Energy, Space, and Time for Beginning Scientific Thinkers*. Chicago, IL: Independent Publishers Group, 1993.

Bibliography

Asimov, Isaac. *The History of Physics*. New York: Walker and Company, 1966.

Bloomfield, Louis. *How Things Work: The Physics of Everyday Life*. New York: John Wiley & Sons, 1997.

Buchanan, Alfred. *In Motion*. Englewood Cliffs, NJ: Prentice-Hall Incorporated, 1969.

Cullerne, J. P. *The Penguin Dictionary of Physics*. London, England: The Penguin Group, 1977.

Einstein, Albert, and Leopold Infeld. *The Evolution of Physics*. New York: Simon and Schuster, 1961.

Farndon, John. *Energy*. New York: Benchmark Books, 2003.

Feynman, Richard. *Six Easy Pieces*. Reading, MA: Helix Books, 1995.

Gunderson, P. Erik. *The Handy Physics Answer Book.* Farmington Hills, MI: Visible Ink Press, 1999.

Hewitt, Paul G. *Conceptual Physics: A New Introduction to Your Environment.* Boston: Little, Brown, and Company, 1974.

James, Elizabeth, and Carol Barkin. *The Simple Facts of Simple Machines.* New York: Lothrop, Lee & Shepard Company, 1975.

Lafferty, Peter. *Force & Motion.* New York: Dorling Kindersley Limited, 1999.

Motz, Lloyd. *The Story of Physics.* New York: Plenum Press, 1989.

Index

A
air resistance, 24, 32

C
calorie, 14, 18, 29
chemical energy, 30
chemical potential energy, 13–14
conservation of energy, 28–31

E
elastic potential energy, 12–13
electricity, 6, 8, 9, 27, 30, 31, 41
entropy, 30

F
force, 21–22, 24, 31, 33, 34, 41
fossil fuels, 8–10, 28, 41
friction, 24, 25, 27, 32, 33

G
gravitational potential energy, 15–16, 20, 26
gravity, 15, 16, 17, 32, 33

H
heat energy, 6, 9, 14, 17, 29–30, 31, 41, 42

I
inertia, 31–33, 35

J
joule, 17–18, 21, 22, 33

K
kinetic energy, 18–19, 20, 22, 23, 24, 26, 27, 29, 31, 34
kinetic energy–potential energy cycle, 22, 23, 24, 27

L
laws of energy, 28–34, 39, 41
light energy, 6, 7, 10, 30

M
mechanical energy, 20–27

momentum, 35–42
motion, 4, 11, 18, 20, 31, 35, 41

N
Newton, Sir Isaac, 31

P
pendulums, how they work, 22–24
photosynthesis, 6, 7–8
potential energy, 11–18, 19, 20, 22,
     23, 24, 26, 27

R
roller coasters, 22, 24–27
rotational energy, 18, 19, 26

S
solar energy, 10, 42
stored energy, 11–12
Sun, the, 6, 7, 10, 42

T
translational energy, 18, 19

V
vector quantity, 35, 37
vibrational energy, 18

W
work, 6, 12, 17, 20–22, 23, 30, 31,
     33–34
work-energy theorem, 31, 33–34

About the Author

Jennifer Viegas is a news reporter for the Discovery Channel and ABC Australia. She has also written for *New Scientist*, Knight-Ridder newspapers, *The Christian Science Monitor*, *The Princeton Review*, and several other publications.

Photo Credits

Cover © Alfred Pasieka/Science Photo Library; p. 5 © Mark Peterson/Corbis; pp. 9, 26 © Lester Lefkowitz/Corbis; p. 7 by Tahara Anderson; p. 13 © Reuters/Corbis; p. 15 © Larry Lee Photography/ Corbis; pp. 16, 21, 32, 38 by Geri Fletcher; p. 17 © Karl Weatherly/ Corbis; p. 19 © Stone/Getty Images; p. 23 © Mark Antman/The Images Works; p. 25 © Topham/The Image Works; p. 29 © Tim McGuire/Corbis; p. 34 © National Trust Photography Library/Leo Mason/The Image Works; p. 36 © Royalty-Free/Corbis; p. 37 © Adam Woolfitt/Corbis; p. 40 © The Image Bank/Getty Images.

Designer: Tahara Anderson; **Editor:** Wayne Anderson